I and Thou
in the
Here and Now

Stranger, pause and look;
From the dust of ages
Lift this little book,
Turn the tattered pages,
Read me, do not let me die!
Search the fading letters, finding
Steadfast in the broken binding
All that once was I!
—EDNA ST. VINCENT MILLAY
   "The Poet and His Book"

Kay Anderson

I and Thou
in the
Here and Now

For Sheila —
   I'm touched by your caring acceptance.
" Namasta! " (I honor the light within
you!)

Kay Anderson

p. 49

Word Books, Publisher
Waco, Texas

Dedicated
in sincere appreciation and love
to my Family and Friends
who have touched my life
with gentle acceptance.

Contents

Preface

I have written this book for the uncommon common person who seeks a companion's experience and presence along life's way.

By sharing a portion of my personal journey, I believe I reveal the oneness that unites us in much of our living. The problems that confront each of us are similar. Our responses, while varied, arise from similarly basic emotions. By sharing a portion of my journey, I hope to encourage the reader to *be* that person who was born to be. I encourage the reader to be open, aware, spontaneous, courageous, patient and loving. I invite the reader to be warm and responsive in relationships and experiences that say yes to life, yes to self, yes to others.

In a busy era, when negativism abounds, I have written a positive book to be digested bit by bit as capsules of optimism. With a cumulative reservoir of understanding gained through a life of study and experience, I offer simple, practical, useful direction for moving out of the doldrums, the coldness of depression, the turmoil of life. I welcome the reader into an ecstasy of living life well—today and tomorrow and tomorrow.

Kay F. Anderson

Who Am I?

Author Reflections

I drew a large copy of a Piet Hein GROOKS drawing, and hung it on my wall. It spoke for me. It *was* me—a faceless figure perched in contemplation upon the earth, while spinning in the galaxy. The caption reads: I'd like to know what this whole show is all about before it's out.

What indeed is life all about? Is it concerned with rising daily to march forth into the jaws of society's crisis machine? Is life to be spent—like a limited amount of cash—on raising a family, clothing bodies, feeding faces, going to work, watching TV, worrying, gaining excess weight, losing hair, getting wrinkled, sick and weak? I'd like to know what this whole show is all about, before it's out. Wouldn't you?

11

As a matter of fact, I've spent most of my life trying to gain that understanding. I still remember the day I stood in front of my bedroom mirror and stared at myself, a thirteen-year-old, asking, *"Who* am I? Who *am* I? Who am *I?"*

I recall how I lifted an eyelid with my fingers and tried to see behind the eye. I tried to look in through the pupil. I ran to ask my mother the fateful question. "You're my daughter," she replied. "Don't be silly."

But I wasn't being silly. I had just begun the search that took me twenty-seven years to complete. I say *complete* with some reservations, since experience has shown me that nothing is constant. Everything is in a state of flux.

But from where I stand right now, life has never looked better. Now I *know* why I'm happy or depressed or angry or at peace. I know what I want and how to get it. I am no longer flung about in a crack-the-whip fashion by my emotions or by the emotions of others. I am in charge of my Self. Or at least, I can be in charge of my Self. And that's no small accomplishment.

When I say, at least I can be in charge, I am echoing a realization that came to me some years ago. Until recently, however, understanding the matter of choice eluded me. In my personal daily living, in my church work, in community relationships and involvements, I often reminded others of the choices that faced them. I even re-minded myself, but with little effect on them or on me. *Choice* is after the fact.

After the fact that you've experienced an emotion, after the fact that the experience may trigger old responses from childhood days, after the fact that subconscious motivations direct many of our actions, after the facts are all in—then comes *choice*. Denying the importance of relative facts, choices will be withheld, discounted or in some other way be less than valid.

Now that I've waded through the pain—and flown with the joy—that constituted much of my inner growing, choices are being made in soaring numbers and worth.

I have now committed myself to write some of what I've learned along the way. I know I am not alone in the struggle to find meaning in life. I know I am not alone in the desire to be of value, to make a difference to others. I know I am not alone in the desire to love and be loved. It is the universal condition.

To this end, I shall share my life, my gropings, my discoveries, my sorrows and my joys so that we may walk together, neither of us so alone as we were before.

I am a woman, a newly opened bloom of creation. I am a daughter, a sister, a wife, a mother, a friend. I am an active citizen, a person of moral conviction. I am also a new breed of philosopher.

Unrestricted by the walls of some ivory tower, unenhanced by the breathtaking inspiration of mountaintop contemplation, I have found my way amid diaper pails, grocery store aisles, P.T.A. meetings, church dinners, tennis courts, children, marriage, and all of the childhood absolutism that used to restrict and sometimes paralyze my growth toward BEING.

13

Who am I? I am a part of life longing for itself. I am a unique person largely composed of common wishes, common needs and common goals. I am a part of many other people. They are a part of me. I am a part of you. You are a part of me. Together we reach out toward others, for we all are one.

Life can be beautiful—if we care enough about ourselves and others. Either we go forward, or we go backward. There is no standing still. Please come with me. I've found what life's all about—before it's out.

Uniquely You

Be your own thing.

Some people think their value, their uniqueness, lies in
what they do, *what* they accomplish. I have found the
essence of people is most present in their *being*. The way
someone says "hello," or helps with a task, or touches my
hand—therein, I know the Person.

A post card came today from a friend on vacation. "The people here are very friendly," she wrote, but that was only part of the reality. She herself is a warm and open person who looks for goodness, and finds it.

Each of us carries a particular set of colors along life's way, to use in shading all that we see and experience. Pastels, brilliant splashes of red, yellow and blue, or a bucketful of gray. We have a choice.

At a conference, an artist loaned me his eyes until I was able to see with my own.

Marx shared himself and gave me a world of new awareness. Suddenly, common things took on great significance. I stooped to study a dried and crumbling leaf, and saw the sun move through it casting a lacy shadow on my path.

I felt out of place and hesitant as I returned to a high school homecoming program. When a neighbor girl spotted me from the other end of the room, she ran full speed and leaped into my arms. "I'm so glad you're here!"

Spontaneity, openness, the warmth of freely expressed joy—all were mine that night. What a lovely difference one person can make in the life of another.

My friend's presence can be felt in his yard where a well-pruned Bonsai tree sits at the center of a table. I gently touch the soft lush green moss that covers its roots. In his house, there is the warmth and charm of woodwork neatly finished. In the kitchen, small shelves are built into formerly wasted space.

My friend seems unaware that his hobbies and abilities give pleasure to others. In these expressions of his Self, I find the Person.

I drove into the shopping center and found my timid, midwestern mother listening attentively to a grizzled old man with dark-toned skin. As she smiled a polite goodbye to him, the man placed his hands together, fingers pointed skyward, and bowed. "He had such a heavy accent," my mother explained, "I could scarcely understand him. But he talked on and on." "Mom," I explained, "you listened! For those moments with you, he did more than exist. He *lived*."

For me, the sun rose at 4:30 that afternoon. A day truly begins when a person is affirmed!

Grampa is eighty now, and he still leads us on. Though his eyesight and general health are failing, he still holds full responsibility for the house and our ailing Gramma. He doesn't complain or become bitter. He never has complained. He simply does his best and carries his own burdens with dignity.

He blew me a kiss as I drove away today, and it felt like a blessing.

"You're really neat," I told our instructor, realizing my word choice didn't communicate much more than feelings. Without hesitation, she threw her arms around me. "Thank you," she said.

I don't have to be aloof with others, and they don't have to be so humble they deny the giver of an honest gift. It was beautiful to have someone accept my gratitude as intended. Her response surprised me so much I added a superfluous, "No, really, I like you."

The Masked Marauder

Who's who?

To swim side stroke in the sea of life is to look in one direction, to know half of what exists on the surface. To swim side stroke is to keep water out of my eyes while I miss the challenges and satisfaction that lie beneath the surface. To dive into the depths, to cavort and explore and then explode hungrily through the surface is to become conscious of differences, conscious of choices and variations, conscious that I have the responsibility to care for a real Self in all its dimensions.

"What if I look inside and find problems I didn't know I had? I am what I am, people can take me as I am or leave me alone!" Strong declarations! Strong defenses! Strong fears mask the need to gain self-understanding and acceptance. It's the old ostrich approach—pain will go away if I simply ignore it. Or will it burrow its thorny path into my soul?

Why would a person presume there is bad within? Is it the result of "old time religion"? The result of Freud? My experience defies those teachings. I went all the way to the core of me, and I found there were hurts within, but not "badness." I found loneliness, confusion, self-rejection, sadness, an insatiable hunger for love, but no inherent bad.

"Forget the past!"

Not me! My past holds the keys to my soul, to my sickness, to my health. I am not afraid of the depths. I choose to remember and go beneath the surface, to seek and find buried treasure—rusty, corroded or golden.

At a conference, I found myself praising one man for being open and responsive, while I felt threatened by another who was cautiously critical of the group.

What I praise in someone else may be my own favorite trait. What I fear or reject in someone else may be that which I dislike in my Self. Although I sometimes forget, I want to be aware of projecting my traits, my attitudes onto others. I can't know *them*, until I know my Self.

We meet and greet each other with a glance or a "hello." We talk of surface things, and then go our separate ways again—alone.

How stealthily a mask can hide me from the world, from those who love me or could love me. I can think that people aren't interested in my concerns, but what a wall! It's in sharing concerns and dreams and lives that I become whole.

A friend of my childhood now sits before the TV every day, not bothering to change from her nightgown and robe. With vacant eyes and nervous hands, a life withers from within. Now and then a flicker of personhood stirs to bring a laugh or a hurriedly abandoned tear. But, oh . . . once she was alive!

I wonder what guidance she followed? "Put on a happy face." "Be a good soldier." I wonder if life slipped and twisted from her grasp while she hid behind tea cakes and a mask of well-being? I wonder what her life would be like now if she had said, "I hurt. Please help me."

I still remember when my father whirled around in frustration and asked, "Does everything have to have a reason?" I answered him with my teenage defiance, "Yes!"

Early in life, I committed myself to a search that eventually brought reason and rationality to my life. I dug into the motivations for my actions and moods in spite of repeated advice to "forget yourself!"

Getting to Know You

Keep in touch!

Where would we be without mirrors? How else could we see to cover up defects? How else could we know who we are?

There is another way, a more accurate way to "know thyself." *Reflection*—not the silvered reflection in a glass, but a pulsating human reflection—can be found in Self and Others.

With a chosen awareness, I begin to get acquainted with Self. I listen to my tone of voice, catch my reflection in a store window, notice whether or not people respond positively to me. Little by little, I begin to *see*, to *hear*, to *know* who I am. If the reflection is better than expected, I rejoice. If the reflection is negative and disturbing, I may choose to change. But first, I need to get acquainted.

I stood behind a tense and frowning man at the grocery store. When the clerk treated him coolly, with no personal recognition, he confronted her. "What are you so glum about? It would be a lot nicer to shop here if you'd just smile once in a while."

I must remember to look within myself to know the face I show to others. I want to recognize my own reflection when I see it.

Doors slam, tires squeal, voices rise in pitch and power, a fist is clenched, a head aches—symptoms of trouble within.

Actions and reactions. Again and again I have wondered why a certain trouble came to me, why I felt so crummy after an emotional outburst. That "why" has become my invitation to reflect, to get acquainted and remind my Self of my humanness, my limitations, and my potential. I can't afford the luxury of uncontrolled emotion.

We sat side by side, new friends, breaking the barrier of unknown personhood. "What are your expectations of me?" she asked, and her directness shocked me.

But she was right. I did have expectations. I wanted us to know each other, to care about and share both the problems and the dreams of our lives. I hoped she'd be my friend.

I stood at the kitchen counter, spread the bread with peanut butter and began eating while I poured some milk. In one unbroken process, I had my lunch.

Who else would I take so lightly? Who else would I serve so poorly? Then why me?

I drove my daughter to school, said goodbye, and then glanced back to see her waiting to give me one more wave along with a special feeling.

I returned the wave and hoped I had accurately reflected her love. Then I smiled to myself and wondered who was reflecting whom!

In general, people have treated me well. But I didn't accept their reflections. I was convinced that those "others" were not seeing me clearly. I was convinced they wouldn't like me if they really knew me.

So I dug way down, way back in memory, and found that the big bad BAD was GOOD! I was freed from a childhood idea that had plagued my search for acceptance, love and peace of mind. Now reflections from others have more value.

At various times through the years, I've stood beside my mother's friend. If I placed my hand on her arm, she put her hand upon my hand. If I shook her hand, she held mine. If I smiled, her smile lingered with acceptance.

Adults have a precious gift to offer children. To tell a child, through actions as well as words, that I see him as special—that is a reflection of worth.

My friend and I had talked of many things that day, and one remark troubled me. She had doubted her worth as a person.

What did she mean when she said she "hopes" she is a good person? I know too well the devastation of self-recrimination. I can't bear to meet and care about her and know she hasn't seen the Person I see in her. There's a need for reflection.

Hocus
Focus

See the show!

"Step right up and get your free rose-colored glasses.
Supplies are unlimited. Step right up!"

Positivism is a magical boon, a magical point of view that
leads to creative solutions and hope. It's more than
rose-colored glass that tints reality. It's much more. It's
tapping into an attitude, a power, in which situations do
change for the better, and people actually are transformed.

Being human, and therefore limited, we can focus in only
one direction at a time. Hocus focus! What'll it be?
Positivism, negativism, or limbo? I opt for the positive.

"Life is too short to waste time on someone you don't like," I overheard a woman say. And I thought about my conviction that life is too short to lose a single relationship over some misunderstanding.

Show me that "perfect person," and then I will have a friend. In no way will I choose that standard to limit relationships in my life. Maybe the person who annoys me is reflecting *my* shortcomings.

An expectant mother shared her concerns with me. "I hope everything works out all right," she said. "If I can't go through with natural childbirth, I'll be the one to blame."

Blame? I don't believe in it. Within the range of awareness and abilities, I believe most people do what they can do. Blame has no value except to give a negative focus to life. I choose positivism. I do what I can do and make the results work out through rethinking, reevaluation, whatever is needed. *I* am the housekeeper of my mind.

It had been a good day, and I sat waiting for my friend to get her jacket. In the next room, I overheard a bitter man berating America. "I'm going abroad when I retire. The bloody taxes are taking everything I make." A woman's voice countered him: "Every country has its problems." But he was not swayed.

I wanted to tell him to buzz off. Get lost with his resentment. And then I realized my happiness had become tainted. He had a right to his feelings. He had a right to speak. And I had a right to choose my focus. I could have relived the happy day instead of listening to him.

One day my focus cleared, and I could no longer say, "She made me so mad!" She may have done something that frustrated or shocked me, but it was I who chose to be mad. I could no longer say, "He ruined my day." He may have forgotten to do something I asked, but *he* didn't ruin my day.

I wasted much of life blaming others for my reactions. I let so much of life simply happen to me. Yet all the while, I held the potential for positive self-direction.

It's easy to list legitimate grievances against others, like the wife who described her husband as gracious and charming at work, self-centered and demanding at home. Her description was accurate.

But to focus on an offensive person is to lose one's own way toward hope. *I* am the only one who can change *me*. Changing or accepting my condition is *my* responsibility. To keep my focus realistically directed at self-change—that is the challenge; that is the doorway to my fulfillment.

Our whole family settled down to watch a television presentation about rape and the subsequent trial which set a rapist free. About halfway through the program, I left the room.

To feed my body poisonous food would be stupidity. To feed my mind poisonous thoughts is equal stupidity. I identified with the victim. I didn't need to be raped, nor did my daughter who watched to the bitter end and wept. We each have the option to be selective about our intake of food, thoughts and vicarious experiences.

It was March 6 when a writer friend phoned to tell me she had enjoyed my Christmas card. "It's been on my desk all these weeks, and I've been meaning to call you."

I was pleased to have been in her consciousness that long. I was touched that she had kept her focus clear and followed her original intent. Positive feelings don't have to be limited by time.

People were lined across the front of the theater, down the street and around the corner. They wanted to see a movie about exorcism. Though the reviews told of horror and negative emotions which the film evoked, people stood in the wind and waited for their chosen "entertainment."

What gets my attention gets me! I went home and wondered about fear and moral responsibility and people. While I believe I am not inherently evil, I also believe I can generate my own evil from within. I could never claim to be a victim of Satan. It is *I* who chooses my actions, my involvements and my focus.

Get
Off
Your
Back

The enemy within

Someone points out hidden flaws in your personality.
Someone turns away beautiful words of appreciation.
Someone holds impossible standards for your Self.
Someone sets your limitations.
Someone discounts your accomplishments.
Someone accepts and retains a distorted childhood image of
Self.

Are you that "someone"?

I was sincere with my compliments, but my message wasn't accepted. "You're always praising people," I was reminded, as if that lessened the validity of my appreciation.

There is a legion of negative forces in a person's life, in our society. I readily accept—or at least struggle with—the insults, the slights, the injustices that are put upon me. I wonder how deeply I accept, or even reconsider, a compliment? I wonder what makes a frown more convincing than a pat on the back?

"That was a really nice retreat," I was told by several people, and then one negative remark captured my attention and dimmed my joy.

Why does one put-down have more effect than a bushel of praise? Can it be that I still accept the childhood decision "I'm *not* OK"? As I weigh the pluses and minuses of each day, I need to remind myself to read the scale accurately, with Adult understanding.

"That was an excellent presentation," I told the speaker. "It wasn't perfect," she responded. "I forgot one thing."

Would it have been such a risk to say, "Thanks, I hoped you'd like it." Why the high hurdles for Self? Why the starvation diet which denies the right to appreciation? What am I demanding of myself?

I couldn't stop my mouth, so I listened to my words. When my tennis partner complimented my overhead smash, I heard myself say, "Fran taught me that." When she rejoiced at my successful lob, I told her, "That's Lila's lob."

I still haven't mastered the ability of saying, "Thanks," and letting it go at that. But I am ever more aware of how I discount my Self. No matter what I do well, my first inclination is to pass the credit to someone else. Perhaps that is being gracious, but Self needs something, too.

A woman showed me some macrame she had done. "This part isn't right," she said, and showed me a small error. "But it's lovely," I told her.

What impossible standards control lives! I, too, am unwilling to accept defects in my work. Perhaps, in time, that woman and I can taste of the simple joy of doing and being.

I was disappointed that I lost my temper, that I criticized, that I failed in my pursuit.

Therein lies a source of quiet desperation. While trees stand stately and protective in spite of their flaws, while the sun shines with beneficent warmth in spite of occasional clouds, while flowers grow and birds sing to the best of their ability, I despair and berate myself for what I do or don't do, for what I have or don't have, for what I am or am not. Then when I've finished picking my own bones, I might turn to devour my neighbor.

It was just a game of tennis, but the words in my head were powerful. My timing was off. I overreacted and hit a lot of balls out of court. And I constantly criticized myself for my errors. I was still picking at my last fault when I missed the next serve.

That's tennis. My standards as a mother, for example, are even higher. And yet I wouldn't ever be as critical of someone else. Despite my growing awareness, I often forget to forgive, especially myself.

There Goes the Judge

The devil made you do it?

Save me from the scourge
of "judges,"
for they would deny me,
even my Self!

I was exuberant when I returned from the conference, and I gave out hugs like a Santa Claus gives lollipops. "You'd better watch yourself," an older woman cautioned, her face set in resentment.

It troubled me to find my happiness was offensive. It troubled me because I, too, used to stand among the judges, deciding what is or is not acceptable behavior. But the longer I live, the more I know I cannot judge another person fairly.

I took my elderly friend to the shopping center. She, who seldom speaks or responds to others, generated a statement while I parked the car. "Look at her," she said critically, pointing to the woman in the next car who had a puffed alcoholic look beneath her mask of makeup.

What a strong impulse it is to judge, and yet how insidious that trait. It blocks me from understanding. It isolates me from relationships and growth. What a precarious perch buoys up a "judge."

I heard a woman playing *Blemish* as she talked about two friends. She very gently but deftly pointed to their inadequacies, the injustices they could well be convicted of doing. And I thought about myself.

It's almost impossible to give up judging, but when I succeed in seeing others as unique people to encounter, then I know what friendship is all about. Friendship is acceptance, the warmth of humans sharing and growing and overcoming loneliness.

During the gasoline shortage, it took me an hour and a half to drive one block to the gas station. When I noticed one car leaving a gap some distance ahead of me, I became anxious that someone might cut in. I thought about honking or walking up to "take charge."

Shortly thereafter, I realized I had a headache. In my childlike effort to keep intruders out, I had tailed a car so closely, I was breathing carbon monoxide. I eased off and left a gap ahead of me. Will I ever learn to think things through before I judge? It isn't easy.

"That girl's a lesbian," I heard a high school student whisper. "I saw her hug another girl this morning."

I wonder if homosexuality would be such a fear and an encroaching condition if we permitted ourselves the natural inclination to hug and touch and care? Since most children begin life by loving both a male father and a female mother is it so perverse that a person feels warmth and admiration toward a member of his or her own sex? Intimate feelings are not necessarily linked to sex.

This must be one of the happiest times of my life. I am aware and at peace. I am aware of the brevity and beauty of life and people.

I am at peace because I can love where I used to judge.

I met a young fellow at several parties with mutual friends, and he seemed aloof, self-contained, difficult to understand. Then one summer afternoon he charcoal-broiled an oyster and fed it to me. As I trusted him to share his interests, he took me for a canoe ride and on a winter walk, tossing snowballs at kids as we went. He makes a difference in my life!

It takes time to know another person. To negatively judge a multifaceted human is to diminish my Self.

A Gourmet's Guide to Happiness

Savor the flavor of joy!

Over three hundred years ago, John Milton shared his conviction that "the mind is its own place, and in itself can make a heaven of hell or a hell of heaven." We've had three centuries in which to assimilate this understanding, and yet, have we understood the power of a mind?

Our society feeds us gluttonous portions of negativism, and leaves this one-sided diet with scarcely more than an antacid tablet for assistance. Stirring up leftover problems and resentments, a person could manage to keep in a continual state of emotional nausea. With self-righteous confidence, "lack of time" could be reason enough to

45

sidestep fresh knowledge, new insights, acceptance of the okayness of Self and Others.

People need a daily intake of positive thoughts and inspiration just to keep their balance in a blatantly verbal and negative era.

A man who was weighed down with the burdens of our modern world enrolled in my workshop. His mind fed upon TV, radio news reports, the evening paper, and weekly magazines that funneled the world's struggles into his awareness. And he was depressed.

I don't think it's reasonable to be open to all the distress of life. Would I be that cooperative in feeding my body nothing but onions? Onions upset my stomach and make me cry.

"Wow, Mom! What happened?" my daughter asked. "You went into your room crabby and came out smiling and peaceful!" "I read," I told her.

Long ago I learned that my mind is often more hungry than my body. I respect that fact and keep favorite underlined books close at hand to nibble or dine upon whenever I choose.

The conference is long past, and I feel like a child whose hands are still cupped to hold a shimmering bubble that once drifted away on a breeze.

It's hard for me to let go of something or someone that completes me. Although the longing makes me painfully aware of my needs, it also makes me aware of beautiful memories. I choose to *recall* and *remember* the joy. I choose to *reach out* again.

"Beauty is only skin deep," goes the old saw, but I don't believe in slamming something if I haven't tried it. So when a friend advised "stay pretty," at a time when I wanted to dress in blue jeans and a sweat shirt and pull my hair back with a rubber band, I tried her advice.

Again and again, I find my spirit lifted and my attitude changed when I care enough to "stay pretty."

I paid thirty cents for a tattered book on friendship which was sold at a college library sale. In that book, I found a statement that continues to affect my evaluation of relationships: "On the road a light shines on us, and life is never the same again."

I respect each new relationship, and I seek the light of this life upon mine. And I know I will never be the same again.

I have the memory of a letter I received when I was ten. In it, a teacher wrote to me as a friend.

I've heard it said that words are cheap. But to a child, kind words of acceptance and concern are often exorbitantly priced. Because such words were freely given to me, I am aware of their value. My words to children are spoken with love.

When a neighbor lady died of cancer, I searched for something soft and huggable to give her daughter. I went from store to store hugging teddy bears and elephants and ducks until, at last, I found a giant frog with dangly legs and a body as responsive as love itself. And I gave her this small offering of concern.

I was so thankful to find one truly huggable toy, that I wrote a note to the manufacturer. He responded that there are always a lot of complaints on his desk, but my note of appreciation stood alone. He was touched and sent me a soft fuzzy dog that sits here beside me in the writing room. Love has a way of unfolding and unfolding.

Think About It!

My mind's made up.
Don't confuse me with the facts.

It isn't easy to stir up a mind that has abandoned its Self.
Years of inactivity, of passive acceptance, have let the
grayness grow from cobwebs to cables that bind and
restrict the power to think. But the mind is like a muscle. It
can be strengthened through use. The blind acceptance of
dictates from others, from the news media, from voices of
the past might be an insult to you. Give your Self a chance.
Think about it!

"In ten years, we'll all be standing in bread lines," the speaker said, and I felt anxiety rise within me.

It took a few moments before my brain could decipher the message and the implications. Then I was faced with a choice. I could spend the next ten years in apprehension over the predicted crisis, or I could appreciate my food now, live up to my potential Self, and face the food crisis when it arrives.

Some church people are upset about the changes in music. Others are troubled by pantsuits and casual clothes that are being worn to church. In their opinion, a casual appearance "is not proper."

How subtly and strongly we are held in check, paralyzed by the past. Think! Does it matter that I worship, or that I worship as someone else decrees?

It fascinates me that children ride the Ferris wheel, time after time screaming as they go.

Haven't I been like a child on the wheel of life, crying out in frightened glee? If I relax when a particular ride is in motion or when I have no control over someone or something, I avoid useless strain. By choosing my next ride, my next involvement with clear reasoning, I gain control of my "fate."

I found a note in my files that read: "A part of me wants to cry, 'I can't make it. Help me.' And yet another part is repulsed by dependence—for dependence has its price. Either I pay by loss of pride, or I pay by becoming vulnerable. Sometimes I pay the double toll."

It sounded valid several years ago. But who says I lose pride by becoming dependent? Who says it's "bad" to be vulnerable? Not I—not in the here and now. I am happy to have friends on whom I depend, and being vulnerable has not brought me pain.

My doctor moved to a new medical building, and I was baffled as I approached the entrance. I didn't know how to get in. There were no handles on the door, and I presumed there was an electric eye. As I advanced and waited in front of the closed door, nothing happened. I backed off, advanced again and waited for the door to open automatically. Then a woman walked up, pushed the swinging door open and allowed me sheepishly to follow her in.

What a philosophical lesson that was for me! Habit has often limited my response to situations. Reactions have often been used instead of clearly computed actions. One graphic humiliation did a lot for my common sense.

It isn't so much *what* happens. . . .

It's how much I care and *why*.

"Don't fill the bathtub! A couple of inches of water are all you need for a bath." I was raised on other absolutes, too, which I dutifully obeyed. And along the pathway of childhood, I temporarily lost the ability that leads to common sense.

I usually shower, but when I bathe, I bathe in a deep tub with bubbles or oil to ease away the tensions that sometimes take hold. It wasn't easy to fill that first tub, but the choice was mine.

Let
Go

Risk and receive.

Ask a toddler to give up a favorite blanket. Ask a child to
give up cowboy boots. Ask a teenager or an adult to give
up a flashy new car. Then you will have some idea of the
insecurity that affects our lives.

Until people can see Self as being of intrinsic value,
until people can begin trusting Others, they will continue
to reach for and hold on to crutches and controls.

Let go of a favorite judgment or fear, let go of suspicion,
let go of the "I know best" attitude, let go of preconceived
relationships, let go of resentments, to find fulfillment and
meaning in life.

Like a fire that I had planned and tended, my daughter grew and flamed and flashed beyond me. I felt I had lost control in a task that was mine. But out beyond my reach, other people touched her life and tamed the fire until a lovely warmth poured forth—even to me.

I see parenthood, at its best, as a give and trust affair. To hold the reins too tightly is to deny creation of its gift. To think, "I alone have the right answers" is to petrify a virgin forest.

"I like other people fine," a teenager told me. "I just don't pay much attention to what they say. I know what I'm doing."

I recognized that attitude. Until I grew and truly opened myself to others, I didn't see that total independence is an unnecessary outgrowth of childhood. Only when I was able to let new thoughts and feelings gain attention in my life, could I shed my solitary shell and *grow*.

My father talked about a lifelong friend. "She's bitter," he told me, "mad at her father for something he did way back in the past. And besides that," Dad told me, "her father's been dead for years."

It wasn't long ago that I wrestled with my own resentments from the past. Until I was able to accept my Self fully, I too was caught in the futility of wounds that wouldn't heal. Funny how ridiculous some attitudes are when they're lived by someone else.

"You don't have to write," I told a friend. And then I waited for the mailman, for I knew there'd be a letter, but there wasn't any.

I try not to place demands on others. I try not to obligate them to reciprocal actions. But I can't deny that I hope they'll participate in the friendship. Meanwhile, I want to recognize their way of being friends, on their time schedule.

There were tears in her young eyes as she talked and struggled with her feelings for her new husband. My first impulse was to shield her from pain and sadness.

But life has lessons to give, rewards for those who seek. I chose not to deprive her of growth. With love at hand, I stood aside.

Sometimes I wanted to take my young friend and shake away her somber moods. I wanted to lift her face, meet her eyes, feel her smile.

I err when I deny someone the right to have feelings. I err when I impose my needs on others. I want to let go so my friend can BE.

Through the years, I always kept on top of things. If a decision were needed, I made it. If action was called for, I responded. I kept up a pace that grew in fury as I tried to live up to my expectations of Self.

When physical illness forced me to delay action and decisions, I found there was an unexpected reward for letting go of my overconscientious reins. Decisions often make themselves. Often, action is not needed.

My friend was leaving and I wanted to cry. I felt my heart slow to a strong pendulumlike beat as if to slow time itself.

I recognized my long-ago childhood fear of "Don't leave me alone." Then I could smile and say goodbye knowing we would meet again.

Take Off Your Armor

The protection racket's a drag.

Armor is designed for protection which precludes the
fact that there is danger to be faced. But what if the
"danger" is imaginary? What if the "danger" is merely
an inconvenience, a trivial upset, enlarged through the
frightened eyes of childhood?

Psychological armor can be a heavy burden that limits
life, that encases warmth and feelings and potential.
It can be removed, by choice.

I watched a middle-age woman pull away from an embrace that welcomed her. I watched her body grow rigid as she struggled with the unaccustomed acceptance. In spite of her well-enforced resistance, she smiled.

The pain that sears the edges of "acceptable" behavior also forges a prison to house our lonely selves. The edicts were set forth long ago. I question their validity, their purpose, their rightness. Must we adhere to past injunctions even if they cripple us?

His older brother died, and condolences poured in—from a man who had known his grandfather, from a woman who had been a little girl when she shopped at his grocery store, from former neighbors, lifelong friends. He said, "Most people are nice, . . . I think."

What needless pain a person can suffer through the years, while a calloused spirit protects a wounded soul. When love comes again, real love, a person may be too frightened to reopen. But if not *now* . . . when?

A young friend was hard to understand, with his flip
retorts and inscrutable smile. Then one day, for a few
minutes, he truly spoke of what troubled him deeply.

I wondered why it had taken so long in coming? Was he
afraid to trust me? Was the risk that great? I could only
hope he would leave the surface pretense for someone
else. I care for him.

My daughter knew how much I was hurting, how much I
needed her, and she came. She came with gentleness and
understanding. She came to reflect the best part of me, so
that I might see and know my Self and find my way again.

There is no mirror so clear and good as the mirror found
in the life of one who loves me. I need only be open.

I told a friend how nice she looked, and she laughed and told me her dress was old, that she originally wore it during early pregnancy, and that now it bulged in new spots. I think we both wished I hadn't even spoken.

I thought it would have been easy for her to accept my compliment, and yet . . . I also have trouble accepting praise. But I'm learning!

A man explained the "great benefits" that would occur because a conglomerate bought out three of our local businesses. Because his mind seemed closed, I withheld my true feelings.

Was I afraid of losing a point? Now I wish I had dared to take a stand for independent businessmen. I believe the world is diminished when any person withholds positive support of the individual.

I didn't need her or want anything special. Today I phoned my friend because she might need me.

Relationships can get bogged down in the propriety of who phoned last, whose turn it is to entertain, or is one person coming on too strongly. Establishing and nourishing a friendship can be emotionally risky—but it's worth it.

If there had been candy or cookies on a family picnic many years ago, I might never have tasted a peach. But since there were no alternative sweets, I forced my teeth through the repulsively furry skin. And I almost cried at the pleasure of finding such goodness beneath the surface.

I was afraid to trust. My initial contact had been unpleasant, just as it often is in relationships with people. I find I avoid certain individuals because they remind me of someone from the past. Peaches and people can be equally disappointing or exciting. And sometimes I almost cry at the goodness I find beneath the surface.

Save Your Steam

Convert!

Lightning flashed. Thunder rolled. The wind blew. And the rain came. It was an honest process, step-by-step. And it reminded me that anger is much like that storm, with its buildup of fury. But anger is about 90 percent dishonest, intended to mask other more sensitive emotions, or intended to manipulate others. It is energy gone astray, loveliness caught in a trap.

A friend and I discussed the unfortunate fact that everyone is subjected to injustices during childhood. We traced the source of some resentments that had telescoped to affect our own lives.

I realize my growth is limited when I continue to feel anger about an action in the past. However, the dangerous thing about resentment is that it seems so reasonable.

A relative visited me while on his vacation and barbed about my friends and my activities. He taunted and teased me until I lashed out at him. Though my words were crude and inaccurate, my message was clear: "You don't count! You mean nothing to me!"

It took months to decipher that emotional crash scene, but I'm glad I stuck with it. Through my busyness with others, I had indicated that he was unimportant to me. By forcing an explosive response, he had proved he *could* make a difference. What a tragic, roundabout way to say "I love you."

As I grew in personal awareness, I saw that I had been taking responsibility for other people's upsets. I saw that I had erroneously taken offense at their remarks, their coolness.

When I read the title of Laura Huxley's *You Are Not the Target*, I saw things in a new light. Those five words remind me that often I am the chance recipient of negative actions and attitudes. To avoid hooking into the anger racket, I remind myself that I am not responsible for someone else's actions. I *am* responsible for my own.

My husband greeted a long-time acquaintance by calling out his nickname. *"You* may call me *Mr.,"* came an unexpectedly cold and angry response.

Obviously something had offended the man, but he didn't identify it or discuss it, and I was saddened. I am always a bit horrified when a person chooses to barter with relationships. A lifetime is such a pitifully short time to be friends.

I listened to a man and woman talk angrily about the mess
our nation is in. They spoke at length about the problems
caused by the gasoline shortage. "People used to drive along
in their 'isolation boxes,' never meeting anyone unless
they literally bumped into them," she said. "Now people
are phoning each other. People are riding together. We're
being forced back into relationships!"

A point of view can affect our living. If I'm powerless
to change an offensive condition, I still retain the power
to adjust my view.

My daughter stomped through the kitchen trying to get
some action by using anger. "Can we go NOW?" she asked.

My children learn their emotional rackets from me. If left
unacknowledged, these rackets can go on to dominate
still another generation and another with dishonest
emotional controls. I see the reflection of my own anger.
Now I must face the challenge of changing my pattern and
hoping she'll change hers.

My friend explained about the bomb of a letter she received. It listed five restrictive rules to be obeyed when she spoke at the spring convention. "I'll say what I feel, what I've lived, and speak out of what I am," she told me. "They aren't buying my soul!"

She could have been intimidated, obeyed the "rules" and harbored an anger that spawned resentment. But she didn't! She made a decision about herself—"I'm OK." Then she directed the emotion and used it positively to write the foremat to two speeches within one afternoon. I was strengthened by her example.

The Vague Pattern Book

What a fit!

Pretend we're in a psychological sewing class, and I've invited you to become familiar with a particular pattern. I encourage you to evaluate its "rightness" for you, to consider altering it where and if that is necessary. I ask if this isn't the same pattern you've followed before. I want you to wonder if you are in a rut with your choices and actions and repetitious patterns. I am curious to know who else in your past chose a similar pattern of being, doing and responding. If you are not happy with your choice, I cheer you on while you choose an awareness that brings sparkle to your eyes, a smile to your lips, direction and meaning to your life.

A woman held up her painfully crippled hands and told me she wasn't able to do much sewing any more. And I looked, and I cared, and I wondered.

She is a member of the generation that doesn't complain, that usually doesn't share its pain. "Keep busy," has been their guidepost, "just don't think about it, dear." But this time, for a few moments on a Sunday morning, we paused, thought about it together, shared a burden, and grew as people.

One man listens to classical music and gets tears in his eyes. He remembers lying beneath a piano long ago, while his mother played Chopin. Another man is bitterly compulsive at his work; he knows no relaxation other than sleep. He doesn't recognize the phantoms of his childhood that drive him on, chiding, "You're never enough, never enough."

Patterns of living do exist. They do direct lives. I can choose to become aware, to identify, to evaluate, and consciously to change negative patterns of the past.

A friend was apprehensive about an approaching reunion. "They're judgmental, critical," she said, "and I don't want to be with them. I'm afraid I'll go right back and become the same old me."

Awareness of a negative pattern is a key that can unlock the ability to change. And yes, it's easy to slip back into an unwanted pattern. But, with conscious practice, a person *can* change.

I thought a speaker was pompous and fuzzy in his presentation, and I said so. When my friend took offense, I teased her about always protecting the underdog. We laughed, catching each other in our old, patterned responses.

I fight some battles of early childhood again and again— a repetitious discharge of resentment and energy without ever succeeding in putting the old pain to rest. Inappropriate responses need to be examined.

My friend's mother offered her daughter dessert with such urgings as, "What's the matter? Don't you like my strudels any more? You've changed." Later my friend explained, "I always wanted more than her strudels. I simply didn't know how to say, 'I want *you*, Mom.'"

I, too, miss opportunities when I get trapped in patterns from the past. Some people continue to see me as they did in my childhood. If they aren't aware of the growth, it's I who must build a bridge of understanding. I want to be aware and responsive, here and now.

Vesuvius
Vents

Avoid costly blow-ups.

There is a rumbling in childhood that can be distracted
by an ice cream cone, a trip to the park, a movie. But
the rumbling isn't gone. Its turmoil stirs in adolescence,
drives a person compulsively through the early adult years,
and often erupts disastrously in middle age. When
obligations lessen, when there is more time to be alone,
Vesuvius vents its venom of resentment, lost dreams,
boredom and disillusionment.

One woman whined and complained, as usual. An intelligent, capable, energetic and willing person, she's crippled from the past—crippled in spirit, not in body. And she's blind—blind to the heavy shadow of her childhood.

After I've become aware of a pattern in myself, it almost leaps out of others who are similarly distressed. I see people locked in a strangle-hold of limitation trying to obey the absolutes of childhood that don't check with reality, trying to control people and circumstances beyond one's power. "Why won't they help me? Why won't they cooperate?" With a twist of insight, a person would do better to ask, "Why do I require their help, their obeisance?" There *is* an answer, a need to grow beyond a childish Self.

I noticed that one woman had not been attending meetings, and when she did show up she was unusually nervous and eager to leave.

Middle age has a way of wearing thin the brave facade of our youth. There is a point at which we may need to seek help.

A man told me that his father had always wanted him to become a minister, but he became an artist instead. Now in his fifties, he drives himself in his work seeking to minister to others through *his* medium, not yet certain that he's fulfilled his father's dream.

He and I and others have placed excessive demands on Self, all because of unresolved and long-ago, external expectations. To become aware, to be gentle with Self, to accept the kind reflections of others—that is a beginning. The past need not consume us.

As a child, I was introduced to a man with a crippled right arm. I can remember trying not to stare, but sneaking extra looks whenever possible. I remember, too, that I came home, closed my bedroom door, and held my arm in a similar deformed position.

After a lifetime of unrealistic demands on my Self, now I realize I can let my Self feel *with* others in their troubles, but I need not become crippled *for* them.

I invited some very special people to our home. And on the day of the dinner, every time the phone rang, I thought they were calling to cancel.

The anxiety of childhood disappointments stretched over into my present moment distorting my perception of reality. If they couldn't come this time, they could come another day. If they couldn't come this time, there are other friends I could invite on the spur of the moment. I need only become aware of *what* frightens me, and *why*. Then alternate choices appear.

"We won't be so busy after next year," a man told his aging parents, "but this year is going to be wild!" Too often the years blend into one frantic race to escape the hungers that speak in aloneness.

Hearing his statement was like having scales lifted from my eyes. Suddenly I saw myself and others "doing our thing" with a sort of desperation—filling time, surmounting self-imposed obstacles, spending our life-force in retreat from terror. Because of illness, I had to stop. Only then could I breathe deeply of the morning air. Only then did I start tasting, truly tasting food. I touched, stroked, held, and released all manner of life in a peaceful new awareness.

Beware Conditional Love

Don't eat your heart out.

When does it begin? It's such a subtle and silent change.
Perhaps it takes root in the death of innocence, when a
person first recognizes the deceit of a relative or friend.
Or does conditional love sit in full bloom on one end of
the teeter-totter of human relationships? Such playground
equipment offers excitement coupled with inevitable ups
and downs. Only by choice can you and I give up the
"get nowhere" pastime of conditional love. When we learn
to accept people as they are, the real joy begins.

I had lunch with two sisters and was surprised to find I received much more than food. The older sister tried in vain to show how much the other had changed. "You never used to be this way," she explained. The younger sister was equally ineffective with her approach. "You ought to wake up. You're living in a dream world." Beneath their reciprocal attacks, I heard each of them saying, "I'll love you *if* . . ."

I gained new understanding. That same conditional love was what I had offered my own family, past and present. Even more so in middle age, I became terribly frugal with love. "Look how old and wise I am. I've earned the right to withhold love." But what a costly wage is separation! Life goes by so quickly.

He used to be so gentle with me, so eager to share all the special and beautiful things in life. Now he's gruff, critical, ready to spring into rage.

I know he's been hurt by life. And I know that it's my turn now to show *him* the secret joys I've found along the way. I choose to love him—as he is!

The *San Francisco Chronicle* carried an article about a suicide in which a woman jumped to her death, leaving an underlined newspaper clipping in her purse on the bridge. The clipping told of the desperate need some people have to be hugged and held.

Is it such a big deal to give someone a hug? Is it such a social taboo that some people are denied its benefit to the point of death? Childhood hugs and touches will not last a lifetime. And so I commit myself to hug and touch and care for others as though life depends on it—for it does.

We were close friends at one time. We laughed and played together and shared dreams. Perhaps she didn't see me as I am. Perhaps she had other needs. For some reason, she withdrew.

I have experienced both the cause and effect of conditional love. By choice, I have grown to see every person as being unique and of value. Now I seek to love unconditionally. People are spiritual beings.

"I can hardly wait for you to meet my husband," a young friend told me. "You two have so much in common."

"I hope you haven't built me up so he'll be disappointed," I said.

"Oh, no," she assured me. "And if you don't hit it off, that's okay too!"

There is something beautifully refreshing among young people today. The walls of absolutism are tumbling down. At last there is room for differences—even among friends.

I watched the birds pecking seed we had spread upon the patio, and then noticed that one bird was crippled. He hopped about on a spindly leg, while the other was withheld and useless.

I thought how easy it is to feel empathy for a little sparrow. And then I thought how much harder it is to feel with an emotionally crippled human. At times I become irritated, threatened, resentful, when I could care if only I remained aware and loving.

I can still see myself as a child getting off the bus, taking the elevator to a top floor and finding my way to my father's office. When I opened the door, the room was big and smoky and noisy with typewriters, adding machines and talk. And then I spied my daddy. He was tall and trim and handsome. "This is my daughter," he announced proudly. Then he took me down to the coffee shop where he bought me milk and a big oatmeal cookie. "This is my daughter," he told the waitress and other friends.

The memory touches me deeply. He didn't ask why I hadn't worn something else. He didn't ask why my hair was mussed. He accepted me. He was proud of me as I was.

Backing Out Slowly

With choice, control, and tally ho!

Around 500 B.C. the philosopher Heraclitus stood on the bank of a river and contemplated that nothing is constant, all is change. Even the river before him wasn't the same water that was there a moment earlier. All these years later, mankind still struggles with change. I may find myself gone astray in some undertaking and still spend a part of my life compulsively trying to force an elusive continuity. I may find an idea, a commitment out of step, but I may cling to it with eyes closed while a rescue ship of new involvement, new relationships, passes me by. Constancy is not necessarily a blessing.

It was a gradual withdrawal I chose. With him I felt childlike, smothered by his opinions. I needed space and time to grow into my own person. I didn't want to hurt him. I simply wanted a chance to be *me*.

A tree that grows in the shadow of other trees is held in place by its roots. Only by distorting its upward growth can the tree reach out for life-giving light. I, however, can choose to reexamine roots, change positions, initiate action that frees me to BE.

"I'll be quitting in September," I wrote on letterhead stationery, but my resignation wasn't accepted. "Let us change your job description. Limit your hours . . ."

Praise is a dubious gift if it leads me to deny my convictions, or the pleadings of my weary body. "No one is irreplaceable," the old saying goes, but no one else is me or you. We do have a unique Self, a unique approach to offer. That's all the more reason to listen to one's soul and respect human limitations.

My first exit from organized society came in grade school
when I told the teacher I didn't want to stay in the "Service
with a Smile" group. And then, when I was "out," I
cried and had my mother help me get back in.

There have been many other times since then when I've
detected the feeling of wanting out of some organization
or other social group. And sometimes I've cried. But
I've come to recognize the inner urgings that free me for
other relationships, other experiences. Change is the constant
condition of life. To embrace it is to know fulfillment.

I do a lot of living in my head.

But there are times when I get confused or overwhelmed
or lonely. Then I come out and seek reflections from others.
I come out and give of myself to someone

It's happened before, and it will probably happen again. I begin to be irritated or hurt by some quality in a friend, and I decide it's time to let go of that relationship.

At times I have a tendency to see a *part* as being the *whole*. By backing out slowly, I have time to correct my perception, to adjust my vision. Then I can see if, in fact, the positive qualities don't outweigh the negative.

I saw a golden flower sway with gentle grace while firmly rooted in dark dense soil. From high above, a butterfly was drawn earthward to taste and draw strength, before going on to other flowers.

It reminded me of the times I used to feel like a helpless captive of a dark earth confined to accepting what fate sent my way. But I am not a plant. I need not be limited by twisted roots of my past. I can reach out and touch and be strengthened by knowledge and love.

With This Ring

War and Peace

While contemplating choices, valid thinking, and accepting the uniqueness of another, marriage comes into direct view. With this ring I enfold you, to nurture and assist you in being your true Self. With this ring I'll lead you around by the nose, or keep you in place to do as I say. With this ring, *I thee wed*. The marriage vows indicate the possibility of a divine relationship. Perhaps the magic word is *thee*, for that term is usually saved for a spiritual being of great worth and meaning. And couldn't it be spiritually meaningful to choose union with another unfolding and expanding Self, to love and work and change and give and grow together?

I decided to marry John when I was only ten, because even then he sent off vibes of acceptance and openness. He has never presumed to be my judge. He has loved me as I am.

Some people measure worth by relative comparisons, but how can something so unique as a person be accurately measured against the standards of someone else? Marriage isn't a contest. It's an experience.

"You're lucky you married John," I've been told many times through the years. But that comment slips right off my back. Marriage—any intimate relationship—has as many ebbs and flows as the ocean. I refuse to call it "luck" that the moon moves in the heavens, to call it "luck" that two people nourish each other.

Luck produces envy. Envy produces resentment. Resentment leads to apathy which is where troubled marriages abound.

"If our marriage doesn't work," a young fellow told me, "we'll get a divorce." A giant escape-hatch was a built-in feature of his marriage.

I can't imagine struggling with fear, indecision, and emotional needs when such a decisive *way out* is already built-in. Because John and I married for life, we *try* harder.

I still remember how he raced the motor, wheels spinning and gravel flying, when he took me on a date. That cockiness was only one facet of the same person who prayed on our wedding night and thanked God for our marriage.

It takes time to know another person. It takes time and acceptance of the whole individual. As I embrace a trait here or there, the doors to love swing open.

I think of childhood questions. Is the sky blue? Does a bird sing? Will the sun shine? Are there rainbows?

Aren't some people seeking the impossible in marriage? Will there be problems? Will there be temptations? Will there be injustices? Will there be loneliness? Will there be joy? Will there be fulfillment? Will there be union? Sometimes. Nothing is constant—even in marriage.

In one marriage, the wife is depressed and disillusioned while the husband is successful and quite satisfied. In another marriage, the husband is weary of his job, the problems with his teenage children. While he is depressed, his wife leaves him.

A "good marriage" needs *at least* one partner to be concerned and willing to work for harmony between two people of different, but equally valid, tone. One person can make a difference, not by changing the mate, but by changing Self.

We were having a family birthday celebration, and I told about my fear when I found our hamster trapped in the heat vent. "But John came through in a crisis," I said, and we all laughed, except John. He shook his head. Without a smile, he repeated in disbelief, "so I came through in a crisis."

Sometimes my words are like misguided missiles. I meant to pat him on the back, but my words were double-edged. I had counted past problems with mice, hamsters, spooky noises, etc., as crises, and John had sometimes failed me. But he has seldom failed in the real crises of finances, emotions and family concerns. I hit him dead center, and he hurt. And I grew in awareness.

It's such a simple thing to let a pat on the back linger to massage a tired shoulder muscle, to rub a weary neck and back. And it feels so good.

Marriage can make life easier and better in many important little ways.

For twenty years, John has listened to me pour out delight and sorrows and questions. He's "been there" for me, and my growing and knowing flourished. Recently I've begun to see and hear *him*.

For years, my needs were so strong I forgot my life partner had burdens, too. When he doesn't venture his own concerns, I must remember the burdens may exist none-the-less.

Different Strokes for Different Folks

Try it. You'll like it.

A little boy sets a fire and gets a beating when he's caught. Still, he sets another fire. A young girl tends a garden, shares her flowers, and receives hugs and words of praise.

Both of these children are getting attention, one way or another. We all seek recognition—"strokes." A positive stroke can be someone remembering your name, helping with a problem, smiling. A negative stroke can be a frown, a sarcastic remark, a slap. Positive or negative, *strokes tell people they exist*—they make a difference. The kind of strokes you received in childhood may still "feel right" to you. But if you're content with negative strokes, with put-downs or caustic remarks, you don't have to be. You can change your stroke pattern. The best way to get a positive stroke is to give one. Try it! You'll like it.

One woman complains and points to blemishes in others. She commands attention and action. Turmoil is her ever-ready companion. Once, just once, I wish she'd accept a positive stroke. Just once, I'd like to be able to thank her for her help without having my attention directed to someone else's failure.

I can wish, and I can try, but *I* can't change people. Their patterns are within; they seek the strokes they get. They may not have that awareness, but they have and use their power of choice.

"Thanks for listening to me," a young girl said, and we went our separate ways. Actually nothing had changed, and yet, so much was different.

I grew up with a hunger to listen and to understand life. And so I've sat on kitchen stools, on benches in the park, on chairs, couches, beds, and listened. I long to know others, to know who and where they are. Because others have listened to me, I listen and hear. Reciprocal strokes!

A brusque man wants attention, respect, love. He seeks it by dominating the conversation, by railroading his ideas, by standing firmly behind his prejudices. And he gets attention, negative attention—he is shunned, rejected and lonely.

In spite of individual preferences, there is a universal need for love. I can't get love on demand, but I *can* get it by giving it away.

Years ago, my big brother used to follow me with a comb in his hand, smoothing my hair into place. And I loved it! And I loved him for caring.

To this day, I respond positively when someone touches my head with gentleness. I equate the touch with love.

I was introduced to a former Playboy Bunny who couldn't care less whether or not anyone commented favorably on her appearance. Then, when my car wouldn't start, she welcomed a compliment.

She rinsed off the corrosion, put distilled water in the battery, and attached a cable from her car to mine. And the engine turned over. A stroke for automotive know-how brought a fleeting smile to her face.

Disneyland Daily

Fantasy pays off big.

No tickets needed!   All folks enter FREE!
Just stir up a dream, and see what *you* see.

Above all else, people need to retain the ability to wish,
to be in touch with their needs and wants. For wishing,
dreaming, fantasying, pretending can let the creative portion
of the mind bring up solutions, new approaches—hope!
Without hope, people despair. Without dreams and
memories, past pain could remain, unseen, to disturb and
direct the now.

So let your imagination soar. Exercise your ability to wish,
to dream and pretend. *Act as if* you can take a fantasy
trip . . . and you will! *Act as if* you have hope . . . and
you will!

The neighbors were gone on vacation. Since I was a momentarily brave six-year-old, I ventured to play on their swing set. At first, my joy was a borrowed thing that might end at the first approaching footstep. But soon I was pumping the swing to new heights. I was flying. I was free—free of my childhood loneliness. I had lost my Self in a glorious new freedom.

As a child, I took on a heavy load of realism. I didn't pretend like other kids. I didn't read fiction. Movies gave me severe headaches. I compulsively tried to figure things out. And it almost destroyed me. Real things don't always make sense.

The workshop leader took us on a fantasy trip back in time, back to our childhood, back to the house where we lived and grew into being. As I mentally wandered around that distant home, fear grew until I stifled a rising cry of panic. I was so small—and all alone.

There are many pains felt in childhood, many distortions of reality. By trusting to memory, by trusting Adult ability to think things through, a fantasy trip can clear out garbage that lies in decay infesting new relationships, new experiences in the here and now.

An old Benny Goodman record stirred a mist of memories in my mind. I saw my brother sprinkling a waxy substance on the basement floor. I saw him twining crepe paper around pipes and across the laundry chute. I saw his crew-cut hair, and I watched him dancing smoothly in the dim, colored lights. It was his party, but he let me be there, too.

For that moment, I experienced a brief reliving of good feelings and good times with a good brother. I found renewal in my "trip." I found perspective for my Being.

The mechanical car sailed far out on a metal arm that carried our young daughters through a realistic encounter with Snow White and the wicked witch! The witch reached out her hand, and terror split the silence of their ride.

How many times the witch of a childhood fantasy—some long-ago blunder, some long-ago "badness," which they have steadfastly refused to face—reaches out to overpower someone in adult life. Yet if it were faced, if light were poured upon it, it would be seen as the distorted perception of a child's point of view.

I pulled the covers up, closed my eyes, and mentally
climbed into my canoe and paddled far out onto the lake.
There I drifted and sang, while the sun kissed my face
and a breeze played about my back. Being *alone* was not the
same as being lonely.

I was nearly forty years old before I learned the treasure
to be found in fantasy. If I can't get to sleep, or if a
persistent thought nags me, I can relive good memories,
recall good friends. Then sleep and refreshment are mine.

Beyond the Here and Now

Linking into life

"This is it, Pal! The big here and now. Live in it!"

Back off with your here and now! That's more than I can take. I didn't drop fully formed from out of the sky. The palm tree didn't spring up in an apricot grove. Give me a steak, and I might ask if it came from a steer or a deer. I want to know what to expect. Tell me everything I "should" accomplish this week, and I might turn away from you and start planning my vacation. Appear on my doorstep, and I might want to know where you're from and where you're going. Call me "friend," and I'm sure I'll want to know of your *life*, not just the time of day. There's depth from the past, expanse in the future, to soften the starkness of the big here and now.

It was cleaning day, and I saved the living room for last. As I dusted the shelves of books and knick-knacks and memories, the day's weariness fell away from me.

I dusted a china doll from my grandmother's childhood, a dog bank, a clay sculpture, a wine decanter, varied little gifts from family and friends. Each holds a memory, a thread in the fabric of my life. The big NOW is often packed with crises and "musts" and "shoulds." I find stability, continuity, and meaning by keeping in touch with the past.

"I wish I had a car," our sixteen-year-old daughter teased, and went on with other wishes and plans for her future. John and I smiled at each other when she left the room. "I get the feeling the girls aren't going to be with us many more years," he said.

The future, too, holds guidance for our actions in the here and now. Realizing the transiency of life, of parenthood, I am awakened to the fleeting moment. Thus aware, I live and love more fully.

"You certainly look happy," my husband commented as he walked into the kitchen and found me rolling out some pie crust. "It's working so easily," I explained.

I was doubly pleased about the pie crust. First, because it was a successful venture, but more importantly, I was using the recipe given me by a friend's mother. When I use such a personalized guide, it's as if the other person is standing beside me, helping and sharing in my life.

I can see him still, "Mr. Pete," with his balding head, his soft round face with eyes twinkling from behind wire-rimmed glasses. I was three years old when I sat beside him on the mohair couch. I sat and waited, without a word, while he talked business with my father just as he had done many times before. And then he turned to me. "How about a stick of gum?" he asked, just as he always did. I beamed my response, took the gum, and went out to play.

I could count on Mr. Pete. He was a part of the adult world that made sense. Because of his friendship with a long-ago me, I try to make sense to other little children.

Sometimes I wonder how the Person I am came to be. And then I look through old memories and dig into some cherished boxes filled with treasures of the years. A grade school autograph book holds insight and direction. A male teacher wrote, "Keep your smile always. It will profit you much." Another teacher wrote, "Keep love in your heart and you will never fail."

Those were simple times. Simple words. But the words have rung true—in the past and in the present. With that batting average, I'll follow them into the future.

At a recent meeting, someone's laughter rang out melodiously and clear. It echoed a fond, almost-forgotten sound from my past. Last night I telephoned across two thousand miles to talk with my fifth grade teacher who first laughed so beautifully.

I still write an occasional note or place a surprise phone call to someone from my past. "Why do you do it?" I've been asked. "You'll probably never see them again." But I don't have to see them. They are an integral part of my life. Keeping in touch recalls memories, and nourishes me while launching my tomorrows.

Our family friend has driven at least five thousand medical miles during the past year, taking his cancer-stricken mother to the doctor and to hospitals. He spends many days off from work seated in medical reception rooms. He could become bitter, depressed, resentful, but he doesn't. He uses the time to relax, to dream and plan for tomorrow.

The courage of even one person casts light upon my way.

Shake, Rattle, and Roll

Hang loose, love.

Even the flowers yielded to the wind, as I watched the worst rain storm of the year sweep across our yard. The tall eucalyptus trees were a moving wall behind our home, for the wind was in command. I squinted to protect my eyes and ran to keep from getting too wet. I moved the lawn chairs to a protected area and went back inside. And I changed my plans for the day.

There will be storms and dry spells and sudden changes in my emotional climate. There will be times when I must relinquish control. But I plan to bend, duck-and-cover, run, wait, wish, grumble, plan, and then go on, after the storm.

I often write out my thoughts so I can see what I'm thinking. "I turned from you today" I wrote, when a friendship started to change, "lest we handicap each other. Already, I see others I might never have known."

Change isn't necessarily an end to an experience. It may begin a broadening, enriching, challenging expansion of Self. Change can provide welcome space.

I wondered how my former friend could have needs so different from mine. I wondered how she could stand aloof, self-contained, when I knew she was crying inside.

I couldn't remain constant in that relationship, but I can seek to be open and receptive to even the slightest response.

Two people met and knew each other though they had never met before. It happens that way sometimes. Branches from the same tree could have been no more closely related than they.

We had about twenty-four hours to get acquainted. And every hour brought new understanding and growth. Since I want to keep this friendship alive, I find time to send out roots of caring through letters, phone calls, surprises. I have an investment in the future.

What is it? One life is not enough for me? I weep when others weep. I rejoice when they rejoice. Today I met a young person filled with spirit and love. Like a tired relay racer, I want to reach out, place the baton in *her* hand, and cry, "Carry on!"

My cry is tinged with regret that an era is past. I have completed a cycle and am moving on. My cry is tinged with unexpected relief, as well. My young friend has the ability and the will to carry on.

A dear friend didn't want to come to California. She said, "If I have to move, I'm taking the old green couch. I'll just lay down and watch TV." And she did. And, in a way, she died.

Change is a reality we all face. To accept it passively can mean ease of adjustment or decline of the person. Each change requires evaluation, flexibility. Add to that an anticipation of some new good within the change. Then things can turn out allright.

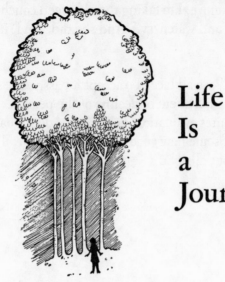

Life
Is
a
Journey

The gentle issue

"What are you going to be when you grow up?" Oh, wow!
That question is a childhood directive that reveals we've
lost our way—postpone your fulfillment, postpone your
happiness, postpone your *being*. But life is not a goal.
It is not an "I'll be happy when" affair. Life is a journey
in which each moment counts. To withhold a smile, a
greeting, a touch, a song, a laugh, a tear, a kind word is
to miss the purpose of the trip. Be! Now!

This morning I stood at the kitchen window and watched a big fat robin fluff his feathers, splash and spread his wings in the bird bath while the sun made sparkles on the water.

A thought shot through my mind, challenging my peace. "Think what you could have accomplished at the typewriter in that amount of time!" There's a slave driver within me, but I choose to defy it. I am not a machine. I want to consciously slow down and take time to feed my spirit on the loveliness within this world.

I have a cut on my hand that glistens as I type. The miracle of healing takes place even while I work. Sensitive new skin is given to me.

How can I be bored or depressed when so many amazing things are happening around me and to me—a wound heals, a heart pumps, food is processed into energy, my lungs expand and contract. Outside my window, the blossoms look like popcorn glued onto branches bare from the cold of winter. Life is an amazing trip. I will not rush it.

Somewhere in childhood, I decided *good* meant doing what I "should." As an adult, a woman struggling with the unfathomable challenges of motherhood, I was forced to learn that *good* means doing and being the best I can.

As long as life remained goal-oriented, as long as happiness was equated with accomplishments, I had only a tentative grasp on joy. When I recognized and accepted my human limitations, I became free to BE as well as to DO.

The gasoline shortage was something more than a burden to bear. It was an opportunity to slow down and BE.

I stayed home more often then. I had time to smell our first lily, and I found Easter's past, sunrise services, candy eggs, bunnies to pet and hold. Springtime! All in a flower.

I phoned a friend at her office and hurried the conversation so I would not interrupt her day. "I want you to know about the camp scholarship that's being offered by the Youth Foundation," I rushed to tell her. "Could we hold that a minute?" she answered with gentleness. "How are you?"

As with a sunrise, a streak of lightning, a rainbow, my feelings were swept to a surprising height by a friend's awareness and concern.

It was warm that day, really warm. And yet my dog snuggled his furry black body close to my side while I rested.

It seems that all forms of life—plants, animals, people— need *touch*. It might be only the touch of warmth—anything but cold isolation.

"Look there!" my friend said, and pointed in my tea cup. I presumed he meant a speck of dust or some lint. "It's okay," I assured him, and poured myself some tea. Then he had to take another cup to patiently show me a heart-shaped reflection that the sunlight cast in the cup.

At least for now, it takes a conscious effort for me to remain silent and receptive. I would like to give others time to reflect, to share, to be.

The birch trees were the whitest I'd ever seen, and I paused in my walking to BE a while with the birch.

To be a part of nature, I need only pause and *experience the oneness* in open reception. I kissed the birch when I left. It was still warm with the afternoon sun.

My day of playfulness is over. It's spent. I walked and talked and laughed with my friend.

And now my soul is full.

Let the Kid Play

Don't miss the fun!

The "child within" is a reality. The most beautiful part of each of us is the Child, the Person we were *born to be.* And yet, that child-part was a bit too wild, impudent, hostile, impulsive, and so we were molded and modified to "fit in" to society.

"There have to be restraints!" True, but it's tragic to lose the Child completely. Within each of us is the potential for laughter, warmth, exuberance, creativity, joy. When emotional hurts get too big, when work gets too rough, when solutions defy you, nurture the Child within. Let the kid play!

117

Our family had gone to the mountains to ski, and one night we all went for a walk in the moonlight. It was a wonderland, with snow banks ten feet high edging the road. "Have some snow," my daughter said, and brought a mittened handful toward my face. "Don't!" I stopped her quickly with a motherly threat that implied she had better not put that snow in my face.

Then I remembered reading an article about the way people grow old, as they shut the door on experience after experience. "Wait," I called after my daughter. "Let me taste it." And it was good. "Again!" I said, and used her hand as a scoop to bring a second taste from the fountain of youth. I made a precious choice, just in time.

I talked to myself all the way to the restaurant. It wasn't *reasonable* to be having breakfast downtown with friends. The day's schedule was too busy already. Still I went, arguing with myself all the way.

It wasn't reasonable, perhaps, but it was fun. We shared our plans for the day, retold some fond memories, and laughed together for an hour. And the whole day was good.

I phoned the library reference desk and asked for help in identifying the source of a particular quotation. From the quiet reserve of a librarian's voice came the response, "It may take me a while, so don't hold your breath. You'll come up with a blue face."

It was only minutes until I received the answer, but the unexpected fun of that comment stayed with me. I am refreshed when someone is free to BE. I am encouraged by spontaneity.

I grabbed a paper towel and wiped my dog's feet when he came in from the rain. Then he grabbed the towel and raced off, with me in fast pursuit—around the coffee table, across the entry hall, into the dining room, through the chair legs and back into the living room. Around and around we raced. At last he ran to his bed, the towel tightly clenched in his teeth, and waited for me to try to gain possession.

In the midst of my work, it took a dog to change my pace. I laughed while we ran, my heart pounding. I gave him a hug, teased him once more (making sure I kept the towel), and returned to my desk refreshed.

I remember once during World War II when my brother and I stood in the kitchen with mother. My memory reveals us in a sort of limbo until Mom broke the spell. "We're going to do it," she said. "Even if we run out later." And then she scooped into the rationed sugar and made us a longed-for batch of fudge.

That memory never fails to please me. Mom, who is ever dutiful and responsive to rules, chose to let her childlike urge for sweets join ours. She became one with us! And I was glad.

Getting It All Together

I and Thou in the here and now

If I didn't take time to buy a cake mix, and then decided to cover my error by using a box of pancake mix, *that* would make a difference. If I followed the directions for my "cake," and cut the baking time in half, *that* would make a difference.

Likewise, if I'm not true to my Self and substitute cool aloofness for warmth and concern, *that* will make a difference. If I accept my life as "half-baked," then my meaning, my relationships with people and other life forms in various phases of my living will be affected. THAT will make a difference.

For me, the joy of understanding, growing awareness and improved capabilities *leads me on*. I want to get it and keep it all together. It works best that way!

All around me, there are people. Yet I am alone. Perhaps we are all alone, each longing for a certain "someone else" who isn't near. Yes, we are quite selective about our relationships with others. And often alone.

I used to pin my hope on one specific person and put my happiness on standby. But when I realized other people were doing the same thing, and *I* was not bringing *them* contentment, even for a while, I stepped back to evaluate. Postponing joy is arresting life. I choose to experience the person I'm with.

How beautiful it is to participate in the growth of a new friendship—to know, respect, and love another person.

How humbling and how beautiful to find myself respected and loved in return.

I let the dog out and stood in the doorway. I smiled. Dawn was lifting the darkness of night; the air was fresh and sweet with natural scents. I was glad for the day.

The memory of other mornings—draggy depressed dawns —is still vivid in my mind. Haste used to push me through breakfast and sandwich making and taking the girls to school. Potential wasted. I missed the exhilaration of a deeply breathed morning gift. There could have been shared dreams, a laugh, a sunrise awareness. I'm glad there's still time.

"This country is suffering a moral depression," my eighteen-year-old daughter said last night. "Listen to how the music is changing. It's so smooth and sad and soothing for all the hurt people."

I used to think motherhood was me caring for my children. Now, when I take time to *be* with the girls, I receive and grow *with* them.

My daughter came home from school and started telling me exciting plans she had for the weekend. I heard words and saw her smile, but I wasn't really "with her."

"Being there" for another person sometimes requires that I sacrifice a pursuit, a thought, a feeling of my own. "Being there" demands awareness, conscious choice and commitment. "Being there" is a burst of light into a relationship. Now you see it; now you don't.

The ladybug floundered on her back until I offered my fingertip assistance. And then she seemed content. She wandered the length of my fingers, the breadth of my hand. But for me, the novelty soon wore off. It was time to start dinner.

I put the ladybug on a plant leaf, watched her spread her wings tentatively and take off. Helping another "get it all together" involves commitment. Often it takes more time than I planned. Occasionally I have to help someone transfer to another life support as I withdraw. But I'm always glad when someone can *fly* on his own.

I listened while one woman plied questions to another, and I almost had the urge to make her stop. I still remember how I used to try to find flaws in certain people, and I didn't like myself then.

My motivations are important for me to understand. Although I like to know the background and motivations of others, I don't always *need* to know. I only need to remain open and accepting as I experience another Person.

I stepped out the back door and called for our robin. "Here, Peep. Peep! Come on." And this time he didn't fly to land at my feet. This time he flew from the pine tree, to the roof, to my head where he perched gently, gripping my hair. And then he flew to my shoulder, and the next day he flew away with his friends.

After Peep fell from his nest, my daughter and I took over as caretakers. Through the weeks of frequent feedings and concerns, we grew in relationship with this uncommon friend. But trust and patience were required by all three of us, and especially by Peep, who became one of few robins force-fed on seed—until we learned that robins don't eat seed! In spite of our bungling, he knew we cared and the separation of life forms was overcome.

I was feeling good about myself. Thoughts were computing accurately. My emotions were at peace. I felt better than ever. Then I was awakened at 4:30 one Sunday morning by a rattly noise that came from our heat vent. I thought maybe a dog bone had fallen in, so I moved through the darkness to remove it. I gasped and pulled my hand back in horror. John turned on the light, and a small furry head poked from the vent, its eyes big with panic. I scooped the exhausted hamster to safety, and returned it to its cage.

I went back to bed, but not to sleep. I thought what it would be like to breathe super-heated air. I thought what it would be like to have bare feet on hot metal. I thought what it would be like to hang on by my teeth, what it would be like to see out but be unable to get out. I lost my perspective. I suffered as if I were the hamster. And I realized how difficult it is to "stay together." I'll have to work at it all my life.

When something disturbs me, I'll save my "Why?" for me.

"Why do you care, Kay? Are you reminded of something in your past?" *My* response is the point to question.

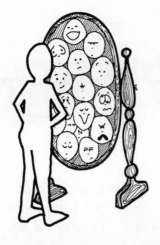

Who
Are
You?

Here's looking at you!

I have tried to imagine you through the months spent in
writing this book. I've tried to separate the pages, to see
you and learn who you are. But I can only guess. Anyway,
the purpose of this book is to help you know you. Still,
I wonder . . .

UNIQUELY YOU

Did you already realize and value *your* uniqueness? I once
read that the way in which a person is different from
others is a most valuable asset. Do you agree?

My differences have often separated me from others.
My differences have made me lonely. At other times, though,

my differences have brought me my greatest joys. They have brought me meaning and purpose and friends and love.

Masked Marauder

What is your experience with personal facades? Do you give others a chance to know you? Or are you wearing a mask? Is it your only false face, your favorite one, or do you have others for various occasions? If you do hide behind a mask, how will I know you? How will anyone truly know you?

Getting to Know You

Who are you? And are you reflecting on your attitude and treatment of your Self? Do you have someone with whom to share positive reflections of each other? If not, why?

Since my high school English class, I have wished for the power "to see myself as others see me." As I've become more open with my Self, so have Others. Reflective insight comes!

Hocus Focus

Have you decided to seek reflections from others? One way to get feedback is to give reflections to those close to you. I recommend positive reflections, at least at first, and maybe always. Negative insights can lead to defensiveness and dissolution of a relationship unless those involved are psychologically prepared to deal with constructive criticism. I have found that I, and others, make the best progress with honest praise.

Do you have a particular focus that is habitual with you? Does it affect the way you see yourself, others, the experiences of life? Is it constructive?

Get Off Your Back

I nearly starved to death on a diet of perfectionism. How about you? Are you able to enjoy what you do, the simple as well as the complex? the failures as well as the successes? Are you able to say, "Well done, Self!" or "Nice try, Pal!" Or do your values get out of balance?

There Goes the Judge

I wonder, too, how *you* deal with the inclination to judge? Personally, this challenge often defies me. But I'm learning. I used to "always be right" with my judgments. Now I'm seldom right!

Have you tried "walking in the other fellow's moccasins"? They never have felt comfortable to me.

A Gourmet's Guide to Happiness

I wonder if you let yourself savor the flavor of a compliment? Or do you rehash the slams and cuts from an angry foe? I wonder, too, if you are sickened by the unnaturally heavy burden of knowing the problems of an entire world? I wonder if you are selective and realistic about the anxiety you hoist onto your shoulders? Do you actually *do something* positive because of your concern?

Do you respond to the hunger cries of your mind and feed it frequently on the wisdom of the ages found in books, in the redwoods, in sunrises and sunsets? What do you do when your mind gets "sick"? Do you drug it, or do you soothe it with music, a walk, solitude? Do you offer your Self some exciting new choices? Or are you locked in a patterned response to the troubles in your mind?

How is your common sense? I didn't have much common sense for years, but it's coming alive now! Do you hassle with rigid values subtly imposed by someone in your past? Are those values worth retaining? Or are they harmful?

Are you frightened, threatened, limited by the absolutes of others? What is it that directs your actions?

Have you grown beyond your own convictions about the meaning of life, the meaning of a person? There's a smorgasbord of choices set before our minds. Are you ready to choose?

LET GO!

Do you see security as a two-faced condition? I see it as an attempt to capture a fresh morning breeze. In it comes! You slam the door, close the windows, and in spite of your efforts, the breeze is gone. Would it be better to enjoy a condition (or a person) while it's near and then kiss it as it flies?

Have you ever wanted to hold the controls on someone else's feelings? I have. But in order to hold, I've learned I must let go. I believe Emerson's statement that "people wish to be settled. Yet, only as far as they are unsettled, is there any hope for them."

TAKE OFF YOUR ARMOR

Who are you? Are you a person held in reserve, wearing armor to protect your Self from harm? Would you rather lose out on smiles and hugs and words of encouragement than to risk being disappointed by someone?

Or are you open, willing to accept the humanness of others, willing to throw off offenses while you cherish the special things people do or have done for you?

Save Your Steam

Are you an angry person—sometimes, often, always, never? Have you studied your Self to see if anger is used to cover up for more sensitive emotions like fear or love?

Accepting the statement that anger is a cover-up, are you the kind of person willing to search out the *real* emotion and deal with *it* instead?

The Vague Pattern Book

Have you become aware of repetitious patterns in your life? Under what conditions do you become angry? Is there a pattern to those conditions? Who in your past expressed their anger much as you do?

What makes you sad? Is there an obvious pattern? Does the motivation lie in your past?

What about struggles with depression, excitement, the blahs? Patterns? If they bind, chafe, hang you up, get rid of them through awareness, conscious choice and substitution of appropriate actions.

Vesuvius Vents

Are you aware of your Self? Do you know some of what made you the way you are today? Do you see similarities between you and a parent? Do you like what you see?

Are you aware of some long-ago hurts that drive you compulsively into activities, tranquilizers, alcohol, sexual excesses, endless work?

Do you ever wonder about *what* you do and *why* you do it? Are volcaniclike pressures building up inside you? If so, what are you going to do about them? Don't get burned!

Beware Conditional Love

Who do you love? And how do you love? Do you show
warmth only if you receive it? Do you give of yourself
whether or not you receive? Or do you keep a balance that
teeters between ups and downs?

Are you aware of the brevity of life? If so, do you dare limit
or withhold your love until a certain specification is met,
until a certain person can receive your love? Remember, love
expands through use.

Backing Out Slowly

I think how much I've changed, even within the past year,
and I think about You. Are you becoming more and more
the person you want to be? Or are you locked in to remaining
the way you "should" be, doing what you "should" the way
you "should." Do you feel you've been "should upon"?
You *can* change. That's your choice.

With This Ring

And in the changes, does marriage come into focus? Are you
————married————single————divorced————opposed
to? And why? Motivations may stretch from the past like a
gigantic rubber band that holds you back, limits your
progress.

Long-ago statements from your parents or other relatives
may be affecting your present experiences or attitudes
regarding marriage. Have you thought about that and looked
for hidden links?

Did someone harm you in the past by words or actions that
now cause you trouble with your mate or with your special
someone? Can you separate facts from feelings long

enough to see who it is you love or don't love and why?
Work at it. It'll come.

Different Strokes for Different Folks

Now I wonder what it takes to make you feel special? Is
there a certain "stroke" you hunger for like touch, shared
experience, growth as a person, excitement, action, solitude?
Do you need ———others———some certain someone
———no one besides your Self to make you feel OK?
(Hey! That's OK, too!) Or do you go for negative strokes?
If you do, OUCH! That smarts!

Disneyland Daily

If life is too heavy or if you're having trouble getting to
know your Self and your motivations, try using memories
or pretending.

If you could be your favorite animal, what would you be?
Where would you be? What would you do? With whom?

Make up a fairy tale, with you as your favorite animal. If
you will do that and take time to look for insight within that
story, you'll find your Self. You'll find you as you've never
seen your Self before! Take a trip!

Beyond the Here and Now

Knowing my Self means *being* my past, present and future.
Do you have any treasures you have saved from your past?
Any memoirs, an old book, a stuffed toy, an award, a pin,
pictures? Do you keep it (or them) where you can see and
touch and remember where you came from—emotionally,
as well as physically?

Have you ever written a plan or a wish for your future? Why not try it, with details? How can you know where you're going if you don't have a wish, a dream, a plan?

You are *more* than you were in the past, *less* than you could be in the future. Keep in touch!

SHAKE, RATTLE AND ROLL

When troubles come or changes that you didn't want, will you be able to roll with the punches? Do you think there could be good in a change that is forced upon you?

How do you face change? Do you act or simply react? Why?

Do you know anyone who has given up on life, overwhelmed by some mysterious thing some people call "fate"? Do you believe in that kind of fate? Please don't sell out to apathy.

LIFE IS A JOURNEY

There are so many gifts that seem hidden on the earth around us. Have you taken time to search for the simple and ever-present joys found in a dew drop on a rose, the sun glistening on a spider's web, the uncurling of a springtime leaf?

All around you is a celebration of life. Have you stopped to watch the wind playing at papers in the streets? Have you stopped to stare as the rain distorts an office window? Have you seen the kindness on one face among the masses? Have you seen the character in a withered hand that grips a cane?

Life is a journey, not a goal. Don't miss the highlights!

LET THE KID PLAY

Work is a major part of life, but so is play. Do you realize that mental health is directly related to the ability to play?

How long has it been since you were silly? Or took the day off to sleep? Or to read? How long has it been since you did something extravagant just for fun?

How long has it been since you ran as fast as you could or skipped or played a game (nonpsychological) or went swimming? Why don't you play more often? To say you don't have time is to qualify for child abandonment! Give the kid a chance. PLAY!

GETTING IT ALL TOGETHER

There is an art to living life well. Have you made progress on getting your Self together? If you've made any positive change toward being more You, give yourself a stroke—a gift, a compliment, lunch with a friend. Will you do that?! And will you take a taste of the I-Thou way of life in which you share relationship with nature, with an artist through his art, with animals and people?

Then you will not be alone, for whether or not we are aware of it, we all are a part of each other. *We are one.*

Fantasy Finale

The Great Escape

After being at a luncheon with friends one day, I came
home to think through the conversations of that noon hour.
I felt frustrated by the lack of fulfillment expressed by
some of my friends. I felt saddened by their willingness to
accept their "lot in life." I felt separated from them when I
shared some of my *flying* experiences.

And then I had a fantasy. Within the fertile garden of
thoughts and wishes and dreams, I saw the birds and
butterflies of the world held captive on the wheels of life.
Though their wings flapped and fluttered, a clasp was closed
around their bodies, and they were seemingly hopeless
captives.

Around and around they went on their particular wheels, pouring out their life force in pursuit of life's daily needs. They were limited to experiences within the scope of that wheel. There they saw their fellow winged beings. There they all dipped down to eat and rest at the end of the day's "journey."

"That's life," I imagined they'd say, just as my friends were saying without actually voicing that conviction. But *I* couldn't bear it! Not for myself. Not for them.

Then into my fantasy came an old butterfly and a senior robin. They had been "flying" for most of their lives. They had seen sunsets over the lake, sunrises on the hills of the forest. They had tasted of flowers and worms. They had climbed to great heights. They had been driven against their will in sudden unexpected squalls. They had taken their chances away from the security of the wheel.

Now they had come home. In a mutual pact, they had agreed to try once more to free their friends from captivity.

"Lift your eyes," the butterfly whispered in a flutter of demonstration. "Look up!"

"Raise your vision," chirped the old robin. "There's more to life than worms. I eat so that I can fly and drift and splash in rain puddles. Lift your heads, my friends."

Still the wheels turned. The lovely creatures remained passively secure within the clasp of life's practicalities. Around and around they *flew,* though I question the use of

that verb. Their only change of pace came at meal times
and at dusk.

On the next morning, the old butterfly visited flowers that
flourished beyond the well-worn and quite barren land of
wheels. And the senior robin sang freely from the branches
of a lush leafy oak.

Perhaps it was an accident. Perhaps it was a plan. But the
uncommon song of the robin caused two birds to lift their
heads suddenly, almost in unison.

With that individual choice, two clasps flew open. Two birds
abandoned the plodding plight of the wheel. The responsive
birds were free, free at last. Together they flew, they truly
flew to join the senior robin. They flew to participate in life.

As if on cue, the old butterfly winged close to one wheel,
settling, lifting, dipping her wings, faltering a bit. She
caught the attention of an eager young captive. Excitedly the
old butterfly fluttered forth toward the blue and waiting
sky. And the young one looked up!

Again a clasp flew open. And for a while the fragile and
untested young wings moved more quickly. Then they
stopped. The wheel moved forward, relentlessly, and the
young one was almost swept away in the down draft.

Just in time, the old butterfly flew close and flapped and
flapped and flapped, until a kindly breeze developed to set
the young butterfly right again. Then away she flew,
up and up and up.

"I'm flying," came the song of the lovely butterfly. "Flying, really flying."

All that day and the next, which would be like years in the life of men, the old butterfly and the young, along with senior robin and his friends, called out to those still trapped on the wheel.

"Look up! There is more to life than the cares of daily existence. Try your wings. Security can be hopelessness. Lift up your vision, your hopes, and you will be set free."

Slowly, one by one, others dared to trust the uncommon call of shared flight. "Trust in GOOD," said the robin. "GOOD created this world. GOOD gave us wings to carry us beyond hopelessness."

And then, late that afternoon, they were gone. These harbingers of freedom moved on to other wheels, to other trapped beings. There was not time to free them all. Life is of the essence. And the essence vanishes.

That was my fantasy. I treasure it. For it gave me the key to unlock limitations that hold and eventually destroy the Spirit that lives in each of us. It showed me that I *do* have expectations of others. I *do* want them to fly.

It's taken me forty years to "get it all together," to understand and assimilate what I've read and heard and experienced. It's taken me twenty years to comprehend the words in Handel's *Messiah:* "Lift up your heads, O ye gates; and be ye lift up, ye everlasting doors; and the King of glory shall come in."

To me, the King of Glory is found in that most beautiful and holy essence called Spirit. It is Life! It is found in the flowers, the trees, animals, streams, and in you and in me. And to have more essence, more Spirit, we have only to lift our sites, lift our thoughts above the routines that hold us securely in place, that would atrophy our wings, our dreams, our potential.

This book, then, is dedicated to LIFE in its fullness of freedom. This book is dedicated to You, with the hope that you, too, will *choose* to lift up your heart and come fly with me.